THE ENGLISH EARTHQUAKE

THE ENGLISH EARTHQUAKE

EVA SALZMAN

BLOODAXE BOOKS

ISBN: 1 85224 177 2

First published 1992 by
Bloodaxe Books Ltd,
P.O. Box 1SN,
Newcastle upon Tyne NE99 1SN.

Bloodaxe Books Ltd acknowledges
the financial assistance of Northern Arts.

Cover reproduction by V & H Reprographics, Newcastle upon Tyne.

Cover printing by J. Thomson Colour Printers Ltd, Glasgow.

Printed in Great Britain by
Bell & Bain Limited, Glasgow, Scotland.

For Frances Salzman,
my folks on Middagh Street,
and in memory of Dr Samuel Salzman

Acknowledgements

Acknowledgements are due to the editors of the following publications in which some of these poems first appeared in Britain: *Ambit, Bête Noire, Encounter, Foolscap, Home and Away: New Poetry from the South,* edited by Carol Ann Duffy (Southern Arts Association/Thamesdown Community Arts, 1988), *London Magazine, Poetry Durham, Poetry Nottingham, Poetry Review, The Printer's Devil, The Rialto, Poetry Wales, Times Literary Supplement, Trees Be Company* (Common Ground/Bristol Classical Press, 1989), and *Verse*; and in the USA in *MSS, Passages North* and *Poet and Critic.*

Eight of these poems were published in Carol Rumens' anthology *New Women Poets* (Bloodaxe Books, 1990).

Contents

9   Promising

10 Power Games

11 The English Earthquake

12 Ending up in Kent

13 Where I Live

14 With Steve Ovett in Preston Park

15 Running Away from Home

16 Station-Waiting

18 The Race

19 Chamois

20 Phantoms

21 Taste

22 Cheap Thrills

24 Rain in New York

26 Sin

27 Parallel

28 There Is Nothing to See

30 Coffee

31 Ode on St Cecilia's Day

32 Closing Time

33 Forcing Flowers

34 Hatred

35 The Refinery

36 Dens Road Market

38 Olympian

40 Egon Takes a Week's Holiday

41 Breakdown

42 Signs

44 Norbert Dentesstrangle

45 Anamorphosis

46 The Usual Seasonal Thing

47 Soliloquy

48 Childish

49 Air Mail

50 Distancing in Wales

51 Belial

52 We Who Have No Country

54 Trompe-l'œil

55 Eden

56   Portholland

57   Seamother

58   Coming to Bed

60   Lunar Eclipse

61   Off Season

62   Time Out

63   Physics

64   Conch

Promising

The proverbial Englishman fondly knows his weather
like he knows his tea, makes his cocksure forecast
by wind-force, dubious light, some nebulous measure,
just as last night's overtaken lovers loved, star-kissed,

and told their innocent lies, meaning every thunderous word.
What is certain about brief rain, cloudy intervals
tongued by a hot sun, the contracts incurred
by unpredictability, those absolute integrals

of weather? Are we certain, lover, that we drive
this rain, or lightning, touching with our fingertips,
or does the timely dramatic flare just bribe
the future, glaze our eyes, while the ringing whips

of rain flail our promises into shape? Artful timpanist,
shots of alcohol light and we're fortune-tellers
paid by ourselves in gold, orchestrating the tempest
as if we'd seized control of Wotan's tiller.

The phone unrings, the bed remakes itself tonight;
if our fingers spark that next electric flash
and thunder still follows that instant of light
let's look down at our bare and promising flesh.

Power Games

The traffic eyes went blank with cataracts,
lorries buckled, the rigid aerial spines
bent for mutant coats – Uri Geller with a blank cheque.

The ant-column of cars wayward and drunk,
all the toy streets had wound down to crime
and accidents, the shops and offices funked.

At home, the TV sizzling like bacon,
we were rehearsing 'I love you' in pantomime –
difficult words for the practised pagan.

Think, that very day we juggled jump-lead cables,
bewildered by the dead car, those precarious lines
we were examining for plus and minus labels.

One false move, those red and blue aortas
could shock you the other side of "live", if misaligned –
the right key, the booby-trapped mortice.

We fell into the pub, sat comfortable in the dark
under currentless bulbs with lame plugs, sipping wine,
negotiating the odd, casual remark.

Then you broke the triangle with that effective
skilful shot; the white flew off the table
as all at once the mains switched on to that collective
'Ah', as if this were first light, the start of time.

The English Earthquake

Somewhere, a cup tinkles in its saucer.
A meek 'oh my' passes down the miles
of manicured gardens, as armies rumble

the monuments of cities continents away.
The budgie chirps 'goodness' to thin air
while Bach quivers slightly and the fat roast

sways in the oven, brain-dead, but chuckling
in its oil. Such a surprise: the settling ground,
innocent with rape and mustard, groaning

under its weight of roses. The premier
sees stars, plumps her pillows for photographs.
Alas, *Watchtower* faces are falling as life goes on

and the Ex-Major winds back years to the war –
its incendiary thrill – his wife flushed
with disbelief as the earth moves unexpectedly,

the giant baby at the core of the planet
rocking its apocalyptic cradle
gently, wailing: 'Hungry, hungry, hungry.'

Ending up in Kent

I'm leaning out the cottage window, latch
unfastened, trying to see for miles, further.
Postcard-picture me in a country of thatch,
twisted lanes, daub and wattle. I entertain
with coal-fires and gas cylinders.
For all through the year it rains, I freeze.
The neighbouring oasts are like spindles,
fat with the wound-up thread of absent summer.
I walk detergent streams, in search of trees.

Someone's put me in a story-book, but kills
every tree before my entrance.
I follow an ordnance map and find
frightening rows of straight and vacant pines.
The earth as barren as the rugs
people in my nearby town put down. Medicine
sting of pine. Listen there, hear nothing. No bird sings.
I'm told that insects are the only living things
in that Forestry Commission flat. And slugs.

Gala-day on the Tonbridge-Hastings line
and my landlord's chopping down his chestnut trees.
Two train stops and you're at a famous waters place
where they renovate shops into sepia prints.
Inside are offices, outside a show of wealth. In me,
when I walk that scenic, cobbled walk, a tall tree
grows crooked, like a money-graph
zigzagging into civic failure. In warm weather
they sell sulphur from the wells for your pleasure.
Good Health! November and the Guy will burn.
What leaves are left on what trees are left will turn.

Where I Live

This is my rinkidink town where the galleon down by the pier
swings on its monstrous hinge, higher and higher
above the Parade and the Palace, the face-lifted Grand,
where the toy bombs went pop and out came the hankies,
the sweet violins: but its front – zipped back up again pronto,
creamy, deluxe – is riddled with elegant spy-holes
where the powerful stare down the sea to a pin-point
rendering it harmless, a piss in a bucket.

On the tarted-up boardwalk, videos sweat and contest
for their sitting-duck targets, after the lights have gone out
finally, late, very late in the night, when the clairvoyant's
left with her ultimate line of deceit; her fatalist streak
has followed her home where the silvery ropes of the slugs
knot infinities over her carpet, trails of the money
she's palmed from the tourists whose luck had already run out.

Bang your spade against your bucket:
Where does anger bed down for the night?
The dolphins go round in their underground circles
of fever, then die. We squat on the shingle

and bang our spades against our buckets,
the westernmost pier now shorn of its land-loving arm,
just like that, not by freak winds or overblown tides.
We're taking our chances elsewhere. The stilts sag down softly
to splayed-out position, punt weakly away from the shore
and the island drifts out to sea, like indifference.

With Steve Ovett in Preston Park

Man makes his spirit strong by lifting weights.
His endurance is beyond belief; he swims channels,
plays rugby, clambers to the North Pole
because it's there (not here) and chugs
along for miles on his own two legs
with 'Rocky' playing in his ear. Hooray!

This statue should inspire us all –
this Brighton man, built of bronze (hard work
has made him) and he pants heroically,
striving, though he's frozen on his pedestal
at the high point of an endless marathon.
Note the artistic strain, the spare frame
with the sinews moulded in overdrive. If he's hollow-
eyed and starving, like a refugee, it's because
the sculptor grew confused along the way.

Joggers of flesh-and-blood pound by on the peace-mile
circuit, in rain or sleet or snow; the will
of man is priceless, artless. Seasons pass
and roses at his feet die back, are pruned,
shoot up again while green corrosive streaks inch down
the cheeks, oxidisation like a macabre sweat;
he's running as hard as he can away from his maker.

Running Away from Home

Do stations make you want to run somewhere –
skip out, tear up your fortunes,
your lot? Your errand is delivery. A luckier one

boards a train, but you aren't going any place
standing there. Trembling with pioneer spirit
you say goodbye to the leavers and kick off home.

'I want! I want!' burns itself on a pyre,
private countries of people passing you by.
Who could ever cross those borders anyway?

The traffic is humming with wishes,
and you want to steer from your obsolescent
destiny, into another. But thank god

life is thrilling constantly somewhere better
than you will ever be. Does it make you want, or want
to want to fly – that jet roar – distant as stars,

passing you over? The trains, the giant planes:
they make you ache to be going. What about the birds
flying, dolphins swimming, the wild animals running

a pot-boiler version of glory you can't shake off,
running from hunters, that great adventure of death,
back to the safety of their known and wild woods?

Station-Waiting

I hear the conductor's whistle
die, this time not for me:
another train easing off from between
the grey-slate platforms. Trains go gently
over fields, at first so slowly
deepening into the woods, their damage
vague, cumulative.
But trains make gladness blossom in me
sudden and hard
when I watch them pass. Aboard
it is another thing, of course.

I wait on a bench, holding
a paper chosen for its easy-
to-turn pages, simple headlines lying
crossways, letters deceptively large,
a box of matches too in hand, on it
a printed swan sailing forth, and far
above my head the sky-
light illusion.

From here it seems
the tracks snake into knots,
bonding for brief lengths,
then dividing, re-meeting further down
the line. I wait.
My train will leave from here
for some direction, rifle
through countryside, the land
unrolling violently, months
unreeling finally. I imagine
a child's coin placed on the rails.
Quickly, the carriage wheels tick over
and it flattens and shines;
once the face is erased,
the element gleams again. Leave-taking

should be swift, a flinging
of self into a great blankness and behind
the screen-door of a lit-porch slams shut. The shock
of that bang should hurry you along.

Folding the paper in quarters I see
the newsprint dyes my fingers black,
words lightening imperceptibly;
its newness smells of chemical.
In an hour I'll throw it away.
The blood-tipped matches come closely crowded.
Only a few will fail; most will light.

The Race

'You can't exactly love a DC10'
he said, huffily, though his hands were blistered and raw
from rope-burns, and they'd lost the wind for their sails.
I too hate planes, their impossible balancing act on air
while laden with fuel, four-hundred hearts.
They trawl a shadow across the continental shelf,
like a pterodactyl's after-image,
a slip-knot in time – the beast raging at extinction.

I swam this summer in the reservoir alone,
leaving him high and dry on the sand behind.
Weightless, I was making for the other shore,
though it was further than it seemed at first.
My wake divorced the water briefly,
but the flight-plan was mapped out ahead of me
already, years ago, invisible, like glass.

Chamois

For all your trouble you could see nothing
but maybe a flurry of choughs like ash
blown between peaks, or another court of orchids
ho-hum by now. Hours climbing the intractable beast
with its pine-hair standing on end,
heartbeat escalating, to reach the heavy hush
of altitude – its welcome numbness.

He clears it, dizzy and foolish
in the wrong shoes; but having left the trees below
he finds a spotless sky, its clouds shrugged off,
with the meadows idle and dozing
and a tacked seam of water dividing
the vertical slope where he finally stops,
happy to have come this far.

Then, he hears the distant scud of light hooves
and the soft tinkling of scree at twice this height –
a far-off sifting of the great from the small.

Totally out of his depth
and his element – the habitual upbraiding
the world gave him – he lights up,
cheerful in the stunningly vacant air
of four-thousand feet, where he's comfortably remote
from the half-bottles of Bells still lying undiscovered
down the backs of sofas and chairs at home,

uncompleted forms stuffed in drawers,
the little jobs he'll weave around, or days spent
furiously waxing company cars to a blank shine.

Phantoms

I should not look for you
where the tide drains out of the marsh,
but under the hidden tufts of grass
where it floods in.
Though there's little reward in tracking down
nature's secrets, still, I follow this walk,
the leak into the ebbing pond,
where the fat pipe sucks moisture
out of the lowlands,
follow the pull through the neck
of the body of water into the currents of bay.
Does that boat pull away the tide?
Does it drag its wake like a fish-catch
or like an enormous anchor of which
it is always trying to be free?
Who drives the motor out of the harbour?
No one to tell me; it has vanished now into the sea.

A blue heron beats slowly out of the rushes
and heavily circles the mud-banks
risen up shining at their lowest hour.
He dives and misses his food;
I turn and go home.
Another day, a dream of you moves me outside to find
the answer it nearly gifted me with,
drives me down the twisted pine-needled path,
its white sand salmon-tinted in the sunset.
A strange light glances off the trees,
hovering just beyond the next leaves.
Behind, the screen door flaps, its poor voice retreats
and the pale house falls into the cover of woods.
I push open the woven reeds that cut,
slosh over the wetlands,
and suddenly stop
half-way through a breath on the desert shore.

Taste

It's Martha's Vineyard, though tide's out for tourists,
and a whole healthy week since they've tied the knot.
Now to work: the firm's line-up, chilled and waiting,
fat corks aching to pop.

She's nibbling untold delights
in the marquee of the host Importers –
sweetbreads, frog's legs, snake.
You know how it sounds like the worst thing
in the world, until you swallow hard.
Then it's not too bad at all,
like chicken really, quite familiar.

Esther's cheque and a Macy's list
tile their kitchen floor with pricey Hex signs –
the emblems of a honeymoon
at a Pennsylvania Dutch idyll of a farm –
which the cat keeps pissing on, inexplicably.

An idea nags at her, a choice: say,
an ugly splat of unchic colour on the walls,
some hang-dog beige, or worse, a brief dream
of institutional green, guaranteed to make her sick.

Cheap Thrills

Picture me as a heroine from some lurid rag,
clothes disarranged,
half-off
following an unceasing flow of adventures
all guaranteed to make your heart beat hard.
Pirates accost me
while I appear unwilling,
but luck rains down on me
at 'The End'
in the form of a hero who hammers lust
into the routine halo.
The tale is completed
with a man and woman glued together
only because your invitation has expired
on that final page
where the words wind up the romance.

Picture me
as a leading lady. It's time,
made-up,
to go out, see friends, take too much drink,
then find the best way to go home
alone. There were so many partners
at the dance, the time I had was fantastic.
Heading back, a man on the train has eyes
for me, I for him.
For a lark,
we indulge in a love-affair
from Fourteenth
Street to Forty-Second
where one of us finally calls it off,
disembarks. At home, the dog
all this time has been sober, left to her own
society, my book open nearby
to the same page too many days running.
Clothes lie
where I left them, trickling out
from under the bed, messily dressing

the chairs, the room. Still desperately
in love with some stranger, I sleep in fits
and starts,
dreaming of the most impossible things.

Rain in New York

A siren sounds.
Oily water runs in the gutters
and you walk through rainbows.
Mica chips fizz underfoot –
you want to scoop them out from the stone –
and traffic-lights like totem-poles
reflect in glass streets.
The residents, not beautiful, are also slick,
test you out,
talk sex and big
and best, bop across the wet road
and take, three steps at a skip,
the sooty stairs down into the subway hole.

Gladiatorial cabbies have it out.
I'm running maybe to see the fire.
Quick, I get in one that says 'For Hire',
ask for the Brooklyn Bridge.
He goes 'Why not?'
Then, racing Angels down the avenue
he turns, says 'Jesus,
the weather's lousy. How's it with you?
Jeez, crime is terrible these days.
The bastards, they should be shot.'

I'd had a mind to ask a stranger back,
but it was someone else's mind put on by mistake.
Something was burning, but what?
Now I speed down Broadway alone,
spinning it out on a run of green
while the sparkling rain pours down,
hurtle past Dave's towards Chambers Street,
splashing red and amber lights like eyes,
the prides of yellow, prowling beasts

I leave behind in my ordinary taxi.
And past the denizens all on heat,
kohl-eyed and carnival-studded,
stunning and striding
like giants onto the dancing floor in my head,
glamorous and vain,
the glitter chips floating in their hair – they're stars –
and sequins on their dress, like rain.

Sin

A flash pool-game, some freak hormonal wiring,
the cab-ride where he gets my drunken yes
and I'm rooked in that dump of a hotel on Forty-Eighth,
that naked room – no secrets but the big one –
with blunt razors studded round a scummy bath,
a dusty portable, no printed matter anywhere,
just a few chairs knifed with the dead initials
of those who went too far, or never far enough.

Parallel

What is my prize possession?
If I said 'My body'
you'd believe me.
But when the lights switch out
and we lie parallel to each other,
nothing meeting,
then our minds wander off
towards what seems the truth.
Then I feel the earth spinning
effortlessly under us,
bearing our weight without trouble,
and I hear the flowers
we planted spring up,
unclasp their robes,
their colours more eloquent
in the night
when they can't be seen.

The word that rose up with me
from a dream,
but fell back,
short of the surface
I remember now.
It was the answer to your question,
but it bears no resemblance
to our living
and our narrow concerns.

There Is Nothing to See

she says, disappointed. Twenty-five cents
into the mechanical binoculars, a quick swivel
to scan the night Manhattan skyline, immense,
but receding, and she resumes the revel

with her boyfriend. The ferry cuts its schism
back and forth, the river behind
re-binding. Another coin
slots into the optical aid; it's advertising,
so have a look. You don't see New York
until you see through the machine,
pay good money for a real view – though our lady
is shrouded, scaffolded, only dimly lit with the vaguest
shadow showing through and nobody
really home underneath.
Or she might emerge, altered, with a horrible face.
It's 1985. I am home. No great cataclysm

in my absence or return. The ferry thrums back towards Shangri-la,
that vast display of flash and neon-spin,
the mad sparkle, the marvellous
halo of CO gas.
Ahead of me, the glass
steeled towers seem pasted on flatboard,
resting on nothing but diamonded water:
unbelievably grand against the starless sky.

This deck is firm, that Manhattan block more like
an unanchored liner, brilliant and over-chandeliered –
its desperate violins yawing. Ashore, romantic
couples, as if leaned against the railing, embrace,
misty-eyed, admiring the elegant berg of ice.
Gazing at that ship's electric heraldry,
I could hang on its vision of gold, gold
dust or silvery hail, emerald-city
myths or fairy tales. But it might collapse

with a thud, drop like a bomb – or in silence perhaps,
slowly, almost unnoticeably begin to descend,
slink back into dead waters, like the Titanic,
as it goes, no one believing in its end.

Coffee

Alley cats howled about love
outside, besotted terrible strains

as we swallowed it cup by cup
like pain, drop after measured drop

in our cave-like kitchen, smelled that rotten
exotic wood, heard the water sob,

dribble down, hiss and steam.
We filled the empty jugs with night,

coffee, the swirling oils,
threw the sodden filter away

with the dregs, the slag-heap horrors
and started all over again;

clean water drenched the grains
to a peaty, impacted mass

and again we tasted the bitterness,
poured milk and sugar into the black.

Ode on St Cecilia's Day

Lights out, downstairs you wallow
in Wagner. Tossing in bed I swallow
philistine words: Turn off that blasted art.
It sometimes seems as if the cart
goes before the horse
when a soprano's voice
simulates some grand, transcendent part

of love we feel we should attain.
Formal court Baroque
never does the trick.
Far closer to the truth are those deranged
Beethoven late quartets that we both like.
And real-life is re-lived in your brain

as you listen to Mahler – suffering refrains
and marches. A childish tune, warped, sustains
that later piercing note
before finally some hope
or resignation in the ending reigns.

Love's intensified while the music plays –
before too long
we all have 'our song' –
and symphonies repeat the misery-phrase
or even found that phrase for all our loving days
when they are gone.

Closing Time

Do you ever watch the emptying out
of pubs? Like blood from veins?
The suicide of going home, and on

to rooms made strange by darkness,
Wagner? Or are these words too strong
for simple things – the killing off of love?

This pict-o-kit of night is wrong; read TV
for darkness and junk-food for Wagner.
Drama can be provided with the chips.

Spring's patchwork of cheer rubs you
the wrong way? Don't misunderstand
when I say I'm crying for you into my coke.

Forcing Flowers

We are naming hybrids. The next one's
Bastard. It's still possible to make
these new strains up. All the fun's
gone however. You too would like to break me
into what I'm not. We're learning zero
but that things are getting worse, from this
astounding failure to another. Love's missed
because we knew it once. We lie to retrieve it,
hopelessly, with letters and with photos,
pain outweighing pleasure, and still believe,
sure it's not the memory that pinks
it into flower. Leaning over, the erstwhile hero
delicately sniffs: memory *is* a rose.
Now, we keep hothouses. In them everything stinks.

Hatred

You were dreaming of a witch with a withered arm,
the twin headlights of her vision yellowed and split.
She handed you twisted roots on a platter, laughed
and spoke in tongues – shrill backward words, mockery and spit.

Now she works her voodoo on your wax and cardboard
torso; you wake up in a freezing sweat, trying to cough
a weight from your chest, the moon's bulbous glare
exactly opposite, a dangling face with all the features wiped off.

The Refinery

You cannot look at narrow-brush moustaches.
You cannot think about gas-cookers, their ovens
flame-rimmed, the diadem of fire, or hear the bell
when it's done. Or think of teeth, lamp-shades, soap,
the refinery chimney-stacks, puffing cheerfully.

You cannot raise your hand in history class
to ask a simple question; your arm freezes
in a parody of salute. You cannot write 'horror'
because horror is a good film for anyone
with a strong stomach and a taste for gore.

Anyway, the antique photographs are grainy,
have blurred into art – that vaseline trick with the lens.

At dinner you sip the rot-gut wine
and listen to the table-talk – an operation botched
or an ache in the joints the doctor couldn't diagnose.
You choke with rage at the meal, gibbering,
while the devil samples your soul like buttered croissant.

Dens Road Market

*It's a pity that Dante could not be brought back and
compelled to live in Dundee for a little; he would add
a sensational new circle to his Inferno.*

HUGH MACDIARMID

Key of the door,
two and one: twenty-one
and we're through to the musty
indoor market smell, its tobacco and spit

and yellowed decor,
the outdated goods, and the otherworldly drone
of the bingo caller, presiding unjustly
at her horse-shoe counter, where the housewives tick

their lucky sevens
on damp cards. We browse through Book Club trash
and Pat Boone cassettes – the bindled rooms
of scarves and skirts, unstrung rackets, laceless shoes,

the traders in heaven
I guess, or possibly at grass,
their vacant booths like ragged, burlapped tombs
in rows, instead of the usual *Back at Two*s.

Unlucky for some,
one and three. Blind Thirty.

Where's the fun
in that caller's drab and deadened certainty,
her business of numbers, the surprise grave
for that headless Barbi doll I lost? *Kelly's eye, on its own,*

Number One.
O Genie of the five-and-dime, the bargain basement's dirty
cellars, where the thrifty dead can save,
who put all my stuff in this stall? *Here is wisdom.*

That no man might buy or sell,
save he that had the mark or name of the beast
(clickety-click,
six-hundred three score at least)

or the number of his name. Well.
I leave with the cry of 'House' at my back.

Olympian

This year, Tim Lillicrap has failed to actualise
his very own long-jump record from last season
when he broke the previous (indoor) record
of 285 miles from Dagenham High Street
to slightly west of Sheffield –
though it should be said that facilities
were poorish this time, Mr Patel being in bed
with a cold when Lillicrap made his descent
and the missus refusing to make the officials tea.
As you said, Larry, not very sporting
and I can't not agree with you there.

Britain's best hopes are pinned to Agnes McCumsky
whose 1.2 second 1,500 metres in practice
she was thrilled and over the world about.
Boy, she's been mounting that podium
at every chance, since her amazing pregnancy.

To the sprints: what a blinder that was,
no more than a ¼ of a second of action...
frankly, your guess is as good as mine.
Was Jackson on his toes? Did the famous lungs perform?
More to the point, was he even there?
That's a question-mark everyone's asking.
It could be that your man was late off the block,
but who can tell? I've got a theory:
the Canadian switched lanes mid-stream
which would explain the Austrian's disappearance,
not to mention the African's change of skin-colour,
though I'm told that's due to atmospheric disturbance.
But don't quote me on that. Over to you, Larry.

Okay, a run-down on the highlights situation:
in hockey the nil-nil scenario will stay unchanged
until someone scores, which could be soon,
or not. The swimmers looked distinctly unwet,
but only a replay will tell us for sure.
As far as I can see, the pole-vaulters' heads
are in the clouds. So, no interview there.

Well, that's the latest in the ongoing thrills and spills at this year's Games. Tomorrow we'll foreground the discus throw, once we've established a link-up with the Andrex Solar System. Larry?

Egon Takes a Week's Holiday

I was born the year of Plaid Trousers – American calendar –
with a craving for bed-and-bar combos with furry rugs
and a nose for Family Choice spam, museum tins of mushy peas
and all the crispy artefacts to be found in a cellophane bag.

I graduated to carveries, where I'd tackle the chef
who brings me to judge for myself the watery grave
where tomorrow's peas are jiggling in their afterlife
and carrots lie transparent in a bouillon solution.

With a lot on my plate, still I relished this assignment:
a four-square meal at Pizza Hut in Milton Keynes,
its floating tuneless score, a stainless-steel horizon lined
with hopeless vats of drying kernels, hiccups of cucumber.

Sheila leaves her order pad's ideogram of sickness and of health
before she crosses the floral mess through swinging doors;
I note approvingly her green Swiss vest, her paper diadem,
though a pleasant smell of garlic nearly wrecks my commendation.

But it's good and leaden when it comes – a starburst wheel
tagged with limp peppers, red mistakes, a plastic lava of mozzarella.
I phone in my report immediately. They come around with prizes:
bottles of Blue Nun, Piat D'or and some cheesy-flavoured stuff.

Breakdown

The car dies on a nowhere road,
I sit in the silence of no engine
as the sun sets in the rear-view

mirror. Darkness stains everything,
including the dashboard clock
without lit handles or dial. Occasional

twin lamps swim by. But those inside
in perfect working order don't know
how I'm stranded and wouldn't care

as they're definitely headed somewhere
and they're strangers. Like a biblical
tablet, the miles-to sign looms ahead –

the now-long miles I should have covered
writ large and the so-far town by now
I should be in. Letters, numbers falter

in a rabble of angles and beams,
then suddenly leap out clear,
resolved by someone's switch to full.

The soundless collisions of light
and the near-silent swish of cars
going home all seem respectful

of night to me, stuck on this shoulder,
night falling. *There are worse things.* Stars
and a slow coldness grow. Finally,

red and gold wildly flashing, help comes.

Signs

Travelling towards the house where the old lady's
body may still lie, if the undertakers haven't arrived,
I'm overtaken by the drama of turbulent weather, religiose

cloud hunched overhead, crowding down, lumbering across
harmless blue. Shadow, light, lock, unlock – mother-of-pearl inlaid
on a monumental kind of cloud. But even in too bright sun

darkness abides. The sky is freed one moment,
then hail, with a quiet, ringing sound collapses down the next.
The sun returns, yet far-off sheets of rain can be seen, one way

or another. The hints of fiercer red look positively holy –
heaven-sent enactments. The earth's spot-lit! Strong bolts

of sun breaking through the blackest body of cloud
to pierce the ground, like columns. Imagine, everything
sublime: stern robes unfolding and thunder crowns the whole
        production.

Imagine: learning how to pray unhypocritically.

I could be in a church! Or just under a secular sky
I'll call the firmament because it rages, lives up to its name,
though no more, say, than that dry square of dirt, unremarkable,

which itself earns the grander name of earth.

I find the rainbow I've been looking for, and it's only
a quarter part of an arc and weak and lasts
the length of time it takes for me to notice it.

Can I help but see it as some personal sign –
the spirit assimilating? Yet that's why not I looked for it
and I'm an unbeliever in so many wondrous things – meaning-laden,

season-given signs, so easy to find and read, ever-present
signs that seem to be made for us, by us, in the way we think.

Every moment someone dies somewhere else, though rainbows
may not form, nor spectacular phenomena occur
or not, at least, on this side of the world at just

that moment. The sun may set without a fuss, the weather
innocuous perhaps, an irreligious sky above while underneath
the same flowers grow as always. Or it may be freezing

but not unusually dismal, though ice shines and each small event

can assume a message for those left, alive who look around
in disbelief that day when one of their number goes under.
It may happen in-between extremes, during supreme

natural imperfections, uncaptioned by a creed, during unassuming
weather – look carefully – with only its ordinary seasonal
signs of glory – the ones you may never notice.

Norbert Dentesstrangle

Purgatory is the internal combustion of the missed chance.
ARTHUR KOESTLER

On the long haul from France to the North
the big whale of a truck beached itself in Dover,
slewed off the approach-road

and failed, half hiked-up on the kerb.
Letters were smeared down the side
in a queasy mess of faux Cyrillic,

the driver erased, his empty silhouette
waiting in the cab. He's vanished
into the gyratory. Anywhere, but here.

Can you name all the things wrong with this picture?
Lord, those wheels, the stagey viaduct
stuttering over our terrified heads.

Hazards limply tried for orange, managed yellow
as everyone swerved to miss.
You've got to catch these things early:

give or take an X or Y, and you're caught
with more than a foot in the unliving.
You go for a whale and barely make a truck.

Anamorphosis

The priest cannibalises
his holiness and the dead one
whose young hours were star-crossed

dies deeper into his coffin.
But now the Catholic watery crosses
pin the congregation to their knees

while his daughter is crying
most unreligiously. The rich say liturgy
at their own expense; now we the unbelievers

grow confused at the failure of the corporeal,
the surprise of thought, arbitrary fire.
Perspective goes out the stained-glass

window, the mystery sold, the Virgin
looking plastic, like a bad ad.
If we could bury our foolishness

and longing into the ground, it would resurrect
into jokes and books, venial
and real. Our friend would steal a fag

at hospital in the "sin-bin" down the corridor.
This church, a great gymnasium
with pews, seems the most outlandish

sin-bin imaginable. So how does water change
into the sea, blood become breath,
the black cat a fiction

of bad luck? Is it a priest's voice saying:
'See; nature *is* divine'...?
Though so is love, lust, or cigarettes:

and the coffin sinks down
back to its well-proportioned size
as it turns by prayer into grass.

The Usual Seasonal Thing

This is that time of year for ghosts,
gale warnings. The radio list goes around the coast
in its late-night litany of unlikely
areas that only exist in storms –
"imminent" or "rising", the jargon of weather-reports.
Half-lit leaves dance grotesquely, sicken.
I hope some hated politician also looks up
from writing a speech, also has a rendezvous
with fear as the wind rattles her panes.

It's that same old maudlin wind.
Still we grow sad and sentimental.
The bottom drops out of the bucket, flooding
everything: floods of tears at the sight
of a senile wool-seller standing at sea
in the middle of her shop, lost
amongst her thousands of skeins of colourful wool,
her eyesight failing, her mind, yes, woolly.

Thunder rumbling, the sky spits hail and its hiss
says: 'Oh life, oh death, sigh' to all this.
But yesterday through an open window, a ping-pong
ball blew in inexplicably. Gods should
send rain like nails or diamonds down,
but ping-pong balls? Let this be a lesson.

Soliloquy

I'm thinking about how ordinary this day is
except I know that my neighbour's giving birth.
If we didn't know, we'd simply say it's sunny
and let's hope it stays that way for the play
we plan this evening. Last night through the wall
at one I heard their privacy – voices, low
and purposeful, a shifting. But all I really knew
was a crying fox outside the window. Then a dog
howling at it, then more dogs across the field.
Curtains glow with headlights, are dark again
when they've gone. Silence settles back. I lie awake.

Great pain is somewhere else, but today the clock
ticks placidly and the dog yawns. No fox screams
in the daylight. A lone bird suddenly trills at ten.
Is it now? I think. But the signs of nature
do not reflect our solipsistic world. At dusk
the players will gather behind the castle ruins,
well-rehearsed and ready, with the audience
assembled in rows, the programmes rustling.
We've already read the script, yet eagerly
we wait to be shown the effortless work. The play begins.

Childish

I'm swimming in a cartoon,
lazily, under a smiley sun.
Sails, stitched with chunks of colour,
zig-zag into the frame and out,
as outboards blubber a happy song.

Now enter a daytime moon
the criss-cross waves have spun
which floats around my shoulders.
No one I know is about
when suddenly there chugs along

our chubby-faced, old-style saloon.
'Uh oh' goes the little hand-brake
and out steps real life.

Air Mail

Words travel badly.
Unwieldy and hard to fold
into smaller bundles,
they take up far more space
than the grain of their truth would occupy.
Those launched over the ocean to you
careen wildly, collide with other letters,
or return to sender,

packages mauled, shredded and torn into strips.
Few arrive intact.
As a battleground for love, the Atlantic
is too enormous and too romantic-sounding
for the bad language. Daggers rust,
fall useless into the sea.

Take the words: *I love you.*
Disembodied, though tantalising,
they arrive at your hearing.
Anybody might have sent them
to the wrong address.
Or: *I ache for you.*
The *ache* has journeyed long distances,
is tired with itself.
How does one ache for a *you*?
What is a *you* and where?
Take these words: *You do not understand.*

Print them and post them back.
We are just our words.

Distancing in Wales
(for Don)

The clouds have abandoned the earth
to its clarity of rowan berry and heather flower
as if to go away is to elucidate,
learn what we mean by each unloosening hour.

After ribbons of track and trees and macadam,
after the deadening service-station miles,
the sheep seem placed on hills by your warm hand
resting near the inscrutable telephone dial.

The wild bracken, brilliant gorse, the perpetual wind
ruffling that lake of undergrowth
all say 'Forget; your windy life, desires
aren't worth a half a length of rope.'

But love links miles like a telephone,
that ripened silence driven down bad wires
and the abandoned mines, the estuary
could come into life through art, or artless fire.

Or forget archaic riches, the idiomatic sheep,
this language evaporating like steam,
all the place names where you are not;
what they possibly, to me, could mean.

The kite shifts valleys, the relentless river
pours out a song we seem to understand
until one day the language dries up altogether
and we must learn to speak in other lands.

Belial

My neighbours have given birth to a monster
I regret to say. His moon-like pate
glows in the dark like a diabolical nite-lite.
He cuts his milk-teeth on steel, and shrieks
the kind of shrieks which can stop your heart, literally.
He shits mountains wherever he can, moves them too.

Isn't he adorable, croon the harpies from down the block,
cootchie-coo; he sucks their wrinkled fingers dry.

His parents sleep with him in his Alien-papered room
because they are under his thumb
which is as big as the Goodyear blimp.
But when mummy and daddy *have* to go out,
sorrowfully and lovingly, they fasten his furry handcuffs
and wrap him in his terry-cloth straitjacket
which is blue for boys. He bites his mother good-bye.

Then he chews his play-plax, builds Trump towers
and Hefner swimming pools, or DNA with a frightful twist.

Getting home too late that night,
his parents hear him bawl the theme of *Neighbours*
from a block away. They hurry up.
The sitter should have been home hours ago.

We Who Have No Country

Many nights ago
our garden would not wait for morning
and we, until two, then three, turned over
strange entrances to earth.
Uncovering a new history,
we chose only the finest shards of pottery –
copper lustre, swan-necked vases,
burnt red amphoras,
their Greeks at games and war.
Through that night our spades split dirt
and aqua painted seas rose
shimmering into our soiled

hands. Silently, eras cast
out of their tombs
plates imprinted with vague spines,
fossils curled into bedrock
released to the air and warmed by our breath.
Broken towns come into view: iron,
cracked teacups and fragments of porcelain flesh,
a startled eye
discovering in rock small cities,
capitals sunken from sight,
where we might have dwelled and slept,
where minerals flash
in the lap of the deep

earth. Stars disappeared;
black velvet settled over our shoulders.
You lifted grey boulders up
from the crumbling cloak of soil
and proudly rolled them down the corner
like statues fresh from the chisel.
A new continent unfolds.
and its monuments are leaning
towards my empty window screen;
the cracks and grooves I once could read
now seem a foreign tongue,
some ancient looped calligraphy,

a cipher maddening and haunting
each time I try to read your face

again, and below again
all history, inch-by-inch,
is burrowing out,
compelling and making us wish
because it is gone.

Trompe-l'œil

The architrave is classical, the ruins
necessarily distant, drawn from life.

On the trumeau, between the window
and non-window, goes a watercolour,

runny and vague, of a river and old mill.
We must people its banks, have good views.

The mill-owner, watching us, is dead and history
when we turn away. Look what art can do:

marry urban surreal to greenery, the nature
in art being what you choose. Green belongs

on walls, and windows needn't be true.
I am not *deceived* by this picture

of outside and I am not deceiving
anyone in my mansion on the river.

Grand plans! If you lack symmetry or scenery
(and you have the time) paint a window

to look like a window. Make wild art.
But also make your framework strong.

What could be missed are the darkened,
sweaty faces just around the corner, advancing.

A fool says: Pay to wipe the murder
off their faces. They are real.

From a *Sunday Times* 'A Life in the Day' feature: Mr Nicholas Ridley, then
Secretary of State for the Environment, stands before one of his paintings.

Eden

These are lukewarm days.
Even a murder would be better.

All the birds are fussing
about love, and flowers threaten
to bloom. That gingerbread
home I could eat with greed.
Too sweet to live in!

Love is also too sweet.
Just listen to that bad music
always played with love and nature.
Who on earth's directing this?

O bring me religion and strife!
I cannot go on like this.

Portholland

Fast-forward the years – this same inlet the little dipper
still filling, or tipping back its share; our converted chapel
salting up; the odd car's three-point turn. Old and parked

in our chairs, we find ourselves saying 'Tide's out again.'
Of course it is. Though now you're mostly worried by the divers
gone too long, diagonal gold fallen across the row of cottages

and a fire spreading on their Citroën windscreen, the cove
and its boulders swallowed whole by now. In the end, they emerge
but slowly, like a negative bloom: first, the twin black heads,

mouthless and goggled, then the black shoulders and torsos,
flippers last, until they stand there, streaming. They peel down
to sallow English flesh, boast about reserves of air.

Seamother

The black conch reconnects
the plaintive distance: '*Seamother?*

There's nobody here by that name.'
Only afterwards, holding on, I wonder,

and miss the loose, smooth dunes
of the East Coast, its ice-age legacy

of pestled sand hotting up
to an agate-bruised shore,

the gauze tides conjuring summer
from the salted wood of stilts and quays

when a dark-green thrill upends me
and iodine rushes into my mouth.

I imagine him re-dial, coolly,
surer than I of a clear line through.

Here, shoals crackle, the undertows hiss
with a grain not fine enough to burn.

Neither can the slow and gentle manatee,
sadly, be reached at this number,

her mermaid rumours docked,
the temporal spell resumed

though I grip the receiver,
making my calls.

Coming to Bed

When you exhale
one final cigarette
and its last smoke drifts,
dies into the furniture,
the day shuts down.
Only then
when the last notes
of music evaporate
with the thinking voice,
with persistence
and choice...only then
do you slip gently
out of the gravity
of consciousness
into a weightless
sphere of sleep.

I'm already asleep,
airing crops,
and you come down
to meet me in this pasture
that rolls in all directions,
where flowers of ideas
shimmer ghostlike,
seed stars nestled deep
in a carpet of clover
sloping up to sky,
far and near,
where the solid bitter sea
tilts, pours into ambiguity
of green, pales,
then dissipates...

I know
when you arrive;
all meadows
like a scarf
roll up

from the corners
and reassemble
as my form
at your point of entry.
Then we wander off
in separate parts,
side-by-side,
until morning unfolds us
and daylight
breaks us away.

Lunar Eclipse

While scientists are asleep
we are taking the moon in
for our purposes. Our shadows creep

across the disc, like curtains,
but so slow, we hardly guess
until its staring certain

light suffuses to a reddish, tissue glow,
more like what we often hope to see:
the astronomy of the soul.

Off Season

The Spanish waitresses are giggling at us
as they serve the coffee and bread, in a Benasque hotel
between seasons, when few tourists bother the town.
We laugh back, unsure, in our own language –
a marble reredos and mischievous misericords,
sacred and profane, strewn across the table;
the Pyrenees unmasked of snow. One girl takes this postcard boldly,
without asking, pretends to read the English;
another fingers the ragged hole in my sleeve
as if by right, the bit of flesh showing through; laughs.

Somehow we have advertised desire –
that tear perhaps, a tone overheard
and unmistakable in any language, the telling eyes.
Ringless hands allow them intimacy with ours, and the fact
that we shall never return to here, chances are.

Tonight we touch and it happens again,
the walls falling away. I can see them now,
the innocent girls in their kitchen
laughing and stripping for the imaginary skiers.
On TV a matador flourishes his cape, his pride
ridiculous, but, as always, sex is in the air he waves aside
as the crowd roars and he is falling too
with the wounds they have been aching for.

Time Out

Imagine there being no exacting word for time,
there being nothing to waste or save, invent
or slip away. Then who would fight the crime
of its fast passing? I'd take, say, the three-cigarette

train departing half-past-after-the-last-word
which wants saying (and not a moment too soon!)
while the numberless dial of my watch would refer
to a changing mise-en-scène winding from sun to moon,

or some event to an eventual end, when a black 'For Hire'
drives me home on its own good time. *Good* time. For tides
aren't for living by, but are only there to admire
occasionally on trips to the timeless seasides.

Nor do we milk cows, farm a natural time, say to friends:
'I'll meet you at the end of this cooking of rice'
or, more vaguely still: 'You know...when the afternoon ends'.
When? Would I be on time, guided by a smoky feel of night,

when it fell, in my bones – another made-up clocking-in machine?
But how would I measure these purposeful distances run,
or almost run, as the case would more likely seem?
The racers might just laugh or chat at the starting-gun.

Yet I wouldn't think to worry if I were late
for anything, wouldn't care by when which boat
came in. Stockbrokers would forget the date
and leisurely ask if you had the 'time' as a joke.

Some joke, infernal time! Not a word, not well-made policy,
but some black jester's dressed-up devastating game
which lets me put off the proverbial plot, infinitely,
so I could wait here forever before you finally came, or not.

Physics

I'm skiving off again, this time pasting down old family photographs
in strict chronology, with tacky titles (the wasters' trick
I could call work, of ordering a mess in retrospect
to make it count) when I find my grandfather at thirty-six

and picture him, still earlier, clinging to his mother,
who, in turn, has him slung around her neck – a tin-type in a locket –
as they pass through Ellis Island where their bones are checked,
stale bread criminally stuffed in their unfashionable pockets.

There's bread here too. And his son, my father, has popped up
fully-formed in the Natural History Museum cafeteria
with its futuristic, stark formica, the cutlery magnetised
in wild patterns the waitress only dreams about, the interior

like a spaceship, and both looking used to travelling in time.
Though now, at ninety, his love of science is reduced to cranky bursts:
'Cripes, what's the point of everything?' he gruffly asks the air
as his rucked arm encompasses the dumbness of the universe

(words which tell me all I ever want to know about growing old).
So it's odd, this little astral-plane vignette; between the two
a möbius strip unfurls the constancy of the lunch ever to come,
the bread he always ate with every meal untouched, waiting like a clue

on the spartan counter – a planetary jumble of rolls
in a basket, and glimpsed behind the glass of undrunk water
a giant thumb; father and son half-turned in their chairs
expecting momentarily the prodigal daughter.

Conch

My grandmother doesn't hear me call; a white mist licks
her skull. She shuffles out to the jungle-yard
to pin a single greying cloth to the drying rack's
sun-dial spines, the dulling weather-vane
where the fading laundry's years have swung and aired.

The piece of washing turns its only two pages
back and forth, re-read by the wind, water veins
mapping the ground, while shadows throw vaguer
and vaguer epitaphs across the sheets snapping in the breeze.
The woman goes inside, and her door shuts again
into the memory I'll always hold of its splintered frieze.

But my real grandmother's sealed thousands of miles away
in her red-brick house deafened with treasure – bone-and-tulle
dancing skirts, dried quills, the family of bells
lined up in ever-decreasing size, their peals subsiding
to white noise, her shell collection emptying the sea,
vowels bleached on another shore; and from the countless shelves
she's taken her umpteenth book to read in bed, yearning
for me, for the children, her ears burning.